How Smart Police Officers Use Situational Awareness To Improve Safety.

Richard B. Gasaway
Drew W. Moldenhauer

Copyright © 2022
Gasaway Consulting Group, LLC
All Rights Reserved.

No part of this book may be reproduced or transmitted in any form by any means, electronic or mechanical, including photocopy, recording, or any information storage and retrieval system, without permission in writing from the publisher.

How smart police officers use situational awareness to improve safety.

by Richard B. Gasaway and Drew Moldenhauer
Gasaway Consulting Group, LLC
1769 Lexington Avenue North, Suite 177
St. Paul, MN 55113-6522
Phone: 612-548-4424
Situational Awareness Matters!
www.SAMatters.com

ISBN-13: 978-1-939571-15-1

Printed in the United States of America by
Gasaway Consulting Group LLC.

Dedication

To all the police officers who try so very hard
to make good decisions under stressful work conditions.

Disclaimer

The recommendations, advice, descriptions and the methods in this book are presented solely for educational purposes. The author and publisher assumes no liability whatsoever for any loss or damage that results from the use of any of the material in this book. Use of the material in this book is solely at the risk of the user.

Contents

Authors Note 9

Introduction 11

CHAPTERS

1 – What is Situational Awareness and Why Does it Matter? 13

2 – Do Officers Train to Fail? 21

3 – Tips for Improving Situational Awareness Through Training. 25

4 – Know Your Equipment. 31

5 – Context-Dependent Learning. 33

6 – Improving Learning and Recall. 37

7 – Freelancing. 41

8 – Complacency Kills. 45

9 – Fatigue. 49

10 – The Silent Killer of Police Officers. 53

11 – B.R.E.A.T.H.E. 57

12 – Meta Awareness. 61

13 – Hyper Vigilance. 67

14 – Frustration Can Impact Situational Awareness. 71

15 – Assuming or Creating Risk. 75

16 – Distractions and Interruptions. 79

17 – Stop Judging to Improve Situational Awareness. 83

18 – When Budgets Impact Staffing. 87

19 – Active Shooter – Police Officer Response. 89

20 – Active Shooter: Collaborating With Fire And EMS. 93

21 – Active Shooter: The Citizen Response 99

Summary 105

About the Authors: 109

Authors Note

If your officer safety program is successfully preventing officer-involved mishaps we would welcome the opportunity to have a conversation to learn more about how you've been so successful.

If your officer safety program isn't accomplishing your officer-involved mishap prevention goals we would welcome the opportunity to have a conversation to discuss some ideas for how improving officer situational awareness might help.

Rich Gasaway & Drew Moldenhauer
612-548-4424
Rich@RichGasaway.com
Drew@SAMatters.com

Introduction

Please allow us a moment to introduce ourselves and, hopefully, establish a level of credibility that will inspire you to read our book.

Rich Gasaway has served 33 years as a first responder, making high-stakes decisions while managing thousands of high-risk, highly stressful emergencies and crises.

Based, in part, on his experience as a firefighter-paramedic, fire chief and emergency scene commander, Rich shares best practices for conducting rapid situational assessments and he helps first responders develop skills that improve decision making, ranging from routine decisions, to high-stakes decisions made under extremely stressful conditions.

To enhance his decades of practical, in the trenches, decision making experience, Rich completed a Doctor of Philosophy degree in his quest to understand the cognitive neuroscience of how individuals and teams develop, maintain and use situational awareness to improve decision making outcomes.

This is Rich's eighth book on the topic of situational awareness and decision making and his contributions have been featured and referenced in more than 400 books, book chapters, journal articles and online articles.

Drew Moldenhauer has 15 years of Law Enforcement experience with two police organizations in Minnesota. Some of the titles he has held in his tenure are Active Shooter Instructor, Use of Force Instructor, Crisis Intervention Team (CIT) Instructor and Field Training Officer.

Drew is currently an Assistant Professor of Criminal Justice at Bemidji State University and is a full-time licensed police officer that works for the City of Osseo Police Department.

Drew holds a Master's Degree of Science in Public Safety Executive Leadership from St. Cloud State University. He is a Certified Master Instructor for Situational Awareness Matters and has a passion for training his clients on this very important subject.

Additionally, the Situational Awareness Matters team has conducted training for over 700 public safety agencies worldwide, helping their members improve emergency scene safety and high-risk decision making, including first responders serving in:

Atlanta	Indianapolis
Austin	Los Angeles
Baltimore	Minneapolis
Boston	New York
Calgary	Philadelphia
Chicago	Phoenix
Columbus	Saint Paul
Dallas	San Antonio
Edmonton	San Diego
Hartford	Seattle
Houston	Toronto

And fire brigade members serving in:

Amsterdam	Hong Kong
Antwerp	London
Auckland	Melbourne
Beijing	Perth
Brisbane	Sydney
Christchurch	Wellington

Chapter 1

What is Situational Awareness and Why Does it Matter?

Let's start with why it matters. Situational awareness is the foundation for good decision making. It stands to reason, the better you understand the details of a situation, the better your decision making will be. However, there is an odd contradiction here. You do not need strong situational awareness to make good decisions. In fact, you can have terrible situational awareness – zero, zip, nada – no idea what's going on, and still make a GREAT decision.

We call that LUCK.

There's nothing wrong with having a little luck on your side. But when it comes to making high-consequence decisions, it might be helpful if officers could figure out a way to program out some of the luck and replace it with a skillset. The skillset involves understanding how to develop and maintain situational awareness and how to use it to improve decision making outcomes.

Many officers understand, perhaps intuitive, that having situational awareness is important. But most have received no formal training on how to develop it, how to maintain it, how to realize it is being impacted, or how to regain it once it has eroded.

The best place to begin the journey toward understanding situational awareness is with a definition. There are many definitions out there. Mine is a hybrid of several with the greatest credit going to the work of Dr. Mica Endsley, one of the early pioneers in the field and, without question, one of the most published researchers on the topic.

> Situational awareness is the ability to perceive and understand what is happening in the environment around you, in relation to how time is passing, and then using your understanding of the situation to accurately predict future events in time to prevent bad outcomes.

To help simplify this wordy definition we would like to focus on the three primary components of situational awareness:

- Perception
- Understanding
- Prediction

Truth be told, the cognitive neuroscience behind how individuals perceive, understand and predict can be a very complicated and messy process to explain. It is neither our goal nor our ambition to provide comprehensive explanations of these complexities. Rather, we would like to keep our explanations simple enough that every officer, supervisor and commander can understand it and immediately apply the lessons in the field.

To help accomplish our goal toward simplicity, we like to use analogies. Developing situational awareness is like building a house. To build a house, you start with a foundation. On the foundation, you build walls. On the walls, you put on a roof. Foundation, walls and roof. This is how we are going to build situational awareness.

Perception – The foundation

The foundation for situational awareness – the start of it all – is perception. Perception is a process by which an officer uses their five senses to gather information about what is happening in the world around them.

Seeing, hearing, feeling, tasting and smelling. Some might argue that perception is the simplest part of the situational awareness development process. All an officer has to do is be conscious, alert, oriented and looking around (i.e., paying attention). And while it may appear to be a simple task, paying attention is not always as easy as it seems.

As you'll come to understand, every component part of situational awareness has the potential to be flawed for various reasons.
How does one perceive the world around them? Officers have five senses. They are always on and always gathering information – Seeing, hearing, smelling, tasting and feeling. The five senses gather information from the environment and send that information into the officer's brain. To briefly explain how this happens, we will use two senses as examples: Seeing and hearing.

To see anything there must be light. In the absence of all light (i.e., in total darkness) an officer will have no vision. There must be light to stimulate the nerves inside the officer's eyes.

The nerves inside their eyes take the rays of light entering through the retina and turn the rays of light into electrical impulses and send those electrical messages into the brain. The brain is a very dark place. Not one bit of light an officer sees actually gets inside their brain. The only thing that gets inside their brain is electrical messages, like Morse Code traveling through a telegraph line.

To hear something there must be sound waves to stimulate nerves in the officer's ears. The nerves in their ears turn the sound waves into electrical impulses and send those electrical messages into their brain. The brain is a very quiet place. Not one sound an officer hears actually gets inside their brain. The only thing that gets into their brain from their ears is electrical messages, like Morse Code traveling through a telegraph line.

The same is true for all of their sensory inputs. To stay true to our desire to keep the process simple to understand, don't think of it as electrical impulses traveling through telegraph lines.

Rather, think of the inputs as jigsaw puzzle pieces. Each of the officer's senses is gathering information – pieces to a jigsaw puzzle – and sending those puzzle pieces into their brain to a destination where the puzzle will get assembled.

Understanding – The walls

The assembly of the jigsaw puzzle is the second part of the situational awareness development continuum – the walls of the house – and that is what we call understanding. Understanding means being able to make sense out of what is seen, heard, felt, tasted or smelled. Some might call this comprehension.

Let's assume for a moment before us we have a thousand-piece jigsaw puzzle we want to assemble. Let's further assume we are not allowed to see the cover of the box. (The cover of the box displays the solution to the problem and rarely will we ever get to see the solution to a problem on the front-end of high-risk decision making.)

The first thing we might do is dump all the puzzle pieces out onto a flat surface, spread all the pieces out and turn them all face up. Spreading the pieces out and turning them face up allows us to see an expanse of information.

Each puzzle piece represents data that can help us assemble a picture of understanding. However, unless we have some kind of mad skills there is no way we can scan our eyes across a thousand random pieces of unconnected information and assemble the puzzle in our head. Rather, we'll need to develop a strategy for making sense of all this information.

In the jigsaw assembly process, as with the situational awareness formation process, we have to start somewhere. And it will be to our advantage, in both efficiency and effectiveness, to make our starting point strategic, versus random.

The most strategic way to start the assembly process for the jigsaw puzzle is to locate the four corners. There is a sound reason to start with the four corners. The four corners represent facts. As we scan the thousand pieces on the table it is nearly impossible to say, with any certainty, the exact location where a piece will end up, except for the corners.

We know, with certainty, the corners will go in one of four very certain places. So, we seek out the four corners and set them in front of us. The corner pieces represent a small number of facts and that is enough to start the process of assembly.

The same strategy holds true for how to assess complex problems in the work environment. Oftentimes there are dozens, if not hundreds, of pieces of information coming at an officer rapidly. If they try to make sense of it all at once it would quickly overwhelm them.

Trying to process too much information all at once can cause an officer's brain to fatigue quickly and make it harder to make decisions.

In fact, it might cause their critical thinking abilities to shut down completely. This is sometimes called analysis paralysis.
So, let's not do that. Instead, let's focus on a small number of the most important, factual, pieces of information. In the case of the jigsaw puzzle, that's the four corners.

Armed with four corners (i.e., a small amount of factual data) we then seek out additional data (puzzle pieces) that fits together with the cornerstone facts. The next most logical puzzle pieces to focus on are the edges because they also contain factual information.

We know, with certainty, the edge pieces outline the puzzle and help to frame – literally – the problem. Then, we start to fill in the information from the edges toward the center of the puzzle. And this is how we assemble our understanding of a situation.

However, sometimes, once we have used up all the available information at our disposal (i.e., all our puzzle pieces are used) there may still be a hole in the puzzle. Some of the important pieces of the puzzle are missing and we must go on a quest to locate them. Missing information in the puzzle causes confusion and, as you can imagine, confusion can cause some serious situational awareness complications.

When the missing pieces of information are located, and snapped into place, we transition from confusion to understanding. This is sometimes called having a "moment of clarity." Clarity relieves confusion and improves situational awareness.

As we try to understand the meaning of our mental puzzle it can be helpful to ask ourselves some questions. The strategy of asking ourselves questions will be used throughout this book.

When it is suggested that an officer ask themselves questions, this is not meant to be a figurative exercise. Rather, it is meant to be a literal and purposeful action. Using the internal voice (called self-speak) to have a dialogue with oneself can help improve all aspects of situational awareness.

For example, ask yourself: "What does this mean?" While an officer may see and hear clues and cues about what is happening around them, it is not always obvious or intuitive what those clues and cues mean.

Oftentimes in fact, an officer is only seeing or hearing the surface clues and cues. There is often a deeper meaning to this surface information.

For example, while carrying on a conversation with someone, there is often a deeper meaning to what they are saying than what is being shared by their words. Sometimes the deeper meaning is implied, sometimes it is assumed and sometimes it is purposely veiled.

Regardless, the receiver of the message will be well-served to be mentally inquisitive about the deeper meaning of the message and to seek additional information and clarification when doubts arise. The same can be said for the visual information an officer captures.

Sometimes everything an officer needs to know is revealed right before their very eyes. But many times, it's not, at least not initially. It may be fully revealed later (i.e., after-the-fact).

But in high-risk, high-consequence environments after-the-fact may mean after the mishap and that is what we are trying to avoid. Officers want situational awareness to help them see the bad things coming in time to prevent bad outcomes.

This requires an ability to look into the future and anticipate events that have not yet happened. Being inquisitive with internal questioning can help officers see and hear information that has not yet been revealed outright.

Prediction – The roof

The most challenging part of the situational awareness development process could, arguably, be a worker's ability to accurately predict future outcomes. In dynamically changing environments where decisions are often time-compressed, it can be difficult to accurately anticipate outcomes. In fact, this is the component of the situational awareness development process most often overlooked and given inadequate consideration.

The process of predication is improved when a worker begins their assessment and decision making process with the desired outcome in mind. Before beginning their activities, workers should ask themselves:

    What does success look like?

    What would failure look like?

What would be the outcome of a good decision?

What would be the outcome of a poor decision?

Prior to taking an action, a worker should mentally envision the outcome of their decision. Then, they should develop an action plan for how to achieve the successful outcome they envision.

What decisions need to be made?

What actions need to be taken?

What is the target objective?

What are the benchmarks to be accomplished along the way that indicates the worker is on the right track?

What could go wrong along the way?

What are the clues and cues – both weak and strong – that would indicate the plan is working or going awry?

The answers to these questions can help a worker develop an appropriate course of action.

Each of the chapters in this book will tie into this definition and explanation of situational awareness. And for the sake of privity, we will not provide an extensive explanation for situational awareness as it is discussed in each chapter.

Chapter 2

Do Officers Train to Fail?

Is it possible to erode a police officer's situational awareness and to train a police officer to fail? Absolutely! I have seen it often. In fact, I still see it at police academies, on YouTube Videos and during police officer training sessions.

There was a time when I didn't see it. In fact, I was one of those instructors who were training police officers to fail. I didn't realize I was doing it. No instructor would train a police officer to fail on purpose. But, accidentally, it's happening all the time and the consequences can be catastrophic.

I remember when I was in the academy and we would do a variety of training to get us ready for our careers as police officers. One of the drills we would train on was felony stops. Felony stops were intended for when we would pull someone over that had just committed a felony level crime or had a felony warrant.

We would first learn to put space between our squad car and the suspect's car. This was to give us more reaction time and create a safe distance from the suspect. We would then exit our squad, take cover behind our driver side door and call the suspect back to us. We would then either have the suspect lay on the ground or kneel. Our partners would come up and handcuff the suspect, search, and secure them in the back of the squad car. The drill would run smoothly, and officers would feel good after it was all done. However, without even knowing it we were training to fail.

How were we training to fail? Well, in law enforcement we learn the difference between cover and concealment. Cover is something we can hide behind that will stop bullets from hitting us (e.g., a brick wall, the engine block of a vehicle).

Concealment is something we can hide behind that bullets can penetrate (e.g., a car door, bushes, sheetrock). In the felony stop drill we were concealing ourselves behind the car door of our squad, which bullets can penetrate. Instead we should be angling our squad cars and hiding behind the engine block of the squad, while giving the suspect orders. We were training to fail, we were placing ourselves behind concealment instead of cover. This could have catastrophic effects if a suspect were to exit their vehicle and begin shooting at us.

Key Takeaways

The lesson here is that under stress, we become creatures of habit. Our brain will instruct our body to perform exactly how we were programmed to perform based mostly on memorization and repetition. This is true when recalling cognitive information (e.g., people's names and email addresses). It is also the case with muscle memory (i.e., the physical movements tied to performing a task). Practice does not make perfect. Practice makes permanent! This can lead to eroding a police officer's situational awareness and in stressful environments police officers can revert right back to how they were trained. Let's train for success not failure!

Everyday life

Think of when you trained a friend or your teen on how to change a flat tire on a vehicle. This training usually takes place in the nice, controlled safe environment, of a clean garage (unless it's our garages). In reality, they will probably be changing a flat tire on the side of a busy road with a lot of traffic cars passing by, often at a high rate of speed.

Have they been trained when it is unsafe to change that tire and call a tow truck instead? If they haven't been trained on this alternate decision, this could lead to poor situational awareness and they get struck by a passing vehicle operated by an inattentive driver.

Discussions

1. Look at your department's training programs. Can you identify areas where you may be training to fail?

2. If you can identify areas where your department is training to fail, discuss solutions so that officers can avoid catastrophic mistakes. Example: Have your officers ever thrown stop sticks during training from behind cover? Remember practice makes permanent.

The most important objective is for police officers to go home at the end of their shift. Training for success plays an important role in improving situational awareness and high-risk decision making.

Chapter 3

Tips for Improving Situational Awareness Through Training

Realistic and repetitive hands-on training

It is vitally important that when training sessions are conducted, the instructor do everything possible to ensure the training is realistic (with consideration for safety and compliance with policies and standards). Every time an officer trains, their brain is learning. The more the training environment mimics the real environment they're going to face, the greater the likelihood their brain is going to recall the lesson through pattern matching.

Repetition helps with information storage and retrieval. It also helps with muscle memory and the ability to perform tasks flawlessly. As the stress levels increase, we become creatures of habit and perform as we are trained. If the training is high-quality and repeated, the chances of high-quality performance under stress are improved. When we train under stress our mind and body retain the lessons better and we will perform better when faced with a real emergency.

Make it emotional

Emotions trigger the release of dopamine which, in turn, aids in the storage of information. When an event triggers emotions, it is encoded more elaborately. This is just a fancy way of saying your chances of recall are vastly improved. Any emotion works. If, for example, you're running an officer-down drill, make the radio traffic as realistic as possible to allow the officers to really feel the stress of the call. When stress triggers emotions, behavior changes too and it is good to practice skills in this altered mental state.

Lessons learned under stress are far more likely to be recalled under stress. This is known as "context dependent learning". Replicate the real environment in the learning environment to improve the memory of the lessons. Setup your scenarios to be as realistic as possible. Use simunition rounds as part of training.

Avoid hindsight bias

When evaluating an officer's use of force incident, whether it is one from your own department or one from another source (e.g., a case study or a YouTube video) be aware you can suffer from hindsight bias. Stated another way, hindsight bias is "Monday Morning Quarterbacking". It is taking what you know about the outcome and then applying your good (often thought to be better) judgment to the situation and coming away believing the persons involved in the use of force incident were not using good judgment in making their decisions.

It is always easy to look at an incident after the fact and find the fault in the decision making. Instead of asking, "Why did they do that!?" change your line of questioning to, "Why did what they were doing make sense to them at the time it was happening?" No doubt it made sense to them at the moment they were doing whatever they were doing. It may not have made sense after the fact, but that is the sort of judgment we want to avoid.

Don't judge

It took me a long time to learn this. Too long, in fact. For years I judged the performance of others based on what I read, heard or saw and rarely if ever, did I take the time to really find out what was happening and how things unfolded. Every officer-involved shooting and use of force incident has a story behind the story. The events that led up to the incident can help fit the pieces together and improve understanding. Some of these back lessons can be gathered from FBI reports but even those reports are often devoid of some of the details and mindsets of the officers.

When you judge others you evaluate their actions using your non-stressed, rational mind. However, when they were making their decisions or deploying their actions they were using high stressed minds and making intuitive decisions. It's not fair to judge this way because we are not, figuratively or literally, walking in their boots to understand what was going on. If you stop judging, you start learning more... a whole lot more!

What-if scenarios

Creating realistic scenarios, either hands-on or in theory, can aid in learning and how to develop situational awareness in police officers. This is a great learning tool and it's not difficult to do. Simply take an incident you have responded to and add a small what-if event to it. We used to do this all the time when we worked night shift and would eat our lunch.

For example, you respond to a domestic scene between male and female roommates. The entire event goes nearly flawless. The training scenario might be, "What if both parties live there but one party has a guest over and the other party doesn't want the guest there? Under these circumstances, what would or should we do differently?" Then talk through the decisions to be made and how the scenario might have played out if the what-if circumstances were present.

Avoid massive or unrealistic what-if scenarios for they will only serve to frustrate the participants and learning might shut down. For example, avoid the "What would we have done if a plane landed on the house while we were responding to the domestic?" Could it happen? Sure... ANYTHING can happen at a scene. But the likelihood is too remote to have a training benefit.

Once officers get good at basic what-if scenarios you can challenge them with circumstances that build in complexity. Just remember to take small steps. Allow the officers to solve the problem. Don't give them the answer. They'll learn more when they deploy their creative problem-solving abilities. Don't hesitate to talk through why various ideas might or might not work.

Putting slides in the PowerPoint presentation

I often use the analogy that training and experiences stored in memory are like slides in a PowerPoint presentation. Each experience, so long as it was stored in long-term memory, is available for recall. Under stress, your brain searches through long-term memory. What's it looking for? Not the complete file of the entire experience. There's too many of those to sift through. It's looking for a pattern match. Something that triggers intuitive judgment about what to do based on past training or experience. Each of these tips: Realistic and repetitive training, making training emotional, avoiding hindsight bias, not judging and what-if scenarios build and store richly coded experiences that can aid in the development of situational awareness.

Advice

When you train, seek opportunities to tie-in situational awareness, building best practices into your scenarios. Never pass up an opportunity to talk about what situational awareness is… How you develop it… How you maintain it… How it can erode… How you'd know it has eroded… and How you can strengthen it once it has eroded.

You can't train too much for a job that can kill you… and at the top of the list should be training on situational awareness. Together, we can make a dent in this problem.

Discussions

1. Discuss how to create training scenarios that are realistic.

2. Discuss creative ways to build repetition into training scenarios.

3. Discuss ways to make training scenarios emotional. It will make memory storage more robust.

4. Obtain a random use-of-force report and discuss what happened. Take special care to avoid hindsight bias and passing judgment on the responders.

5. Create and discuss three what-if scenarios.

Chapter 4

Know Your Equipment

I'll never forget the day we were issued the newest Electronic Control Weapon. As a department we were all very excited and nervous to see the ECW's and we were ready to test them out on training day. ECW's are a critical piece of equipment that allows law enforcement to use a less lethal means of subduing a non-compliant suspect. We were all very comfortable with the previous ECW, we knew this one was different and would take more training. Most cops are not the biggest fans of change especially, when it comes to handing us something more complicated than what we are used to.

The old model ECW was simple, turn it on, point and pull the trigger. This would release the top dart exactly where the laser was pointing, and the other dart would deploy in a downward angle and the spread would be larger the farther the target was away. If the suspect was non-compliant after being hit with the darts, you could simply pull the trigger on the ECW and the suspect would get another ride from the ECW.

The new model had two cartridges and when you pulled the trigger the first time it would deploy just like the old model. However, when you pulled the trigger again the second dart would deploy. We were not used to this and it confused a lot of officers.

To prevent a second deployment from happening, an officer would have to deploy the first round and then hit the black button on the side of the ECW to give the suspect another ride. If the officer accidentally pulled the trigger those darts would go flying wherever the ECW was pointed. This made us very nervous because we knew under stress this would be very difficult to remember.

In a controlled environment we were able to operate the ECW fine, but under extreme stress, I believe a lot of officers would revert back to the old way of training and would have pulled the trigger again causing more darts to fire and possibly cause us to have a use of force issue or shoot our own partners.

Key Takeaways

Situational awareness requires a conscious effort to capture the clues and cues in an often-chaotic environment. When police officers have to focus so much cognitive energy on how to operate their equipment, their situational awareness will be impacted.

Food for thought

New equipment should be used a lot in training to help with muscle memory. Under stress we will revert back to training and if we're using new equipment but haven't trained well with it we may end up using it incorrectly in a hostile stressful environment. These lessons should not be learned on a dangerous rapidly evolving scene.

Everyday life

Think of the time you bought a new power tool. Did it have new or different safety features you weren't comfortable with? Did you take the time to practice with it and framiliarize yourself with it before you used it for its application? What would you do if you were in a stressful situation or if fatigue set in? Make sure you know and are comfortable with your equipment.

Discussions

1. What is the process your department uses to ensure members are familiar with equipment before it is placed into service?

2. Have you ever made a mistake with your equipment under a high stress situation?

3. Have you ever witnessed your partner make a mistake? What did you do to correct this error?

Chapter 5

Context Dependent Learning

As public safety providers, we could make a fundamental improvement in developing situational awareness by looking at how we train. There are some valuable lessons from brain science that can help improve the design of our training programs. One such lesson is "context dependent learning." It has been validated through numerous studies. If you are a training officer, this article may cause you to rethink how to train fellow police officers.

The concept of context dependent learning is fundamentally simple, yet often overlooked in the training of police officers. Essentially, it means if we train police officers in the same environment in which they are going to perform their work they are far more likely to recall their lessons when put back into the same environment on the job.

I remember I had this experience once in the gym I work out at. I remember we were training for an event call "Murphy". It's a very grueling workout that begins with a one mile run, then proceeds with 100 pullups, 200 pushups, 300 air squats, and finishes off with another one mile run. This is all done while wearing a 20 pound weighted vest. We would do this at the gym every Memorial Day.

I can recall doing this workout several times and I practiced and trained for it at Yorfit in Ramsey, Minnesota. I used the same weighted vest, the same pull up bar, and I ran the same route around the building every time. My times reflected this and I got my personal best time while training at my gym and doing the Murphy on Memorial Day.

Fast forward a few months and I did the same workout, only I went to a different gym. I wasn't used to their pull up bar and I didn't know the exact route I was going to run. The lack of familiarity had a huge impact on my times. I had never trained in this environment before and my results showed it.

A more formal research study involved two groups of SCUBA divers. One was the test group and one was the control group. The researchers put the test group in ten feet of water and gave them some information to memorize. They did the same thing with the control group, except the control group was on land. Then the researchers tested the participants by putting both groups in ten feet of water and asked them to answer questions about what they had learned. The group that learned the information while in the water had a remarkably better recall than the group that learned the information while standing on dry land.

This is an example of context dependent learning. It can work while wearing SCUBA gear in ten feet of water, and it can work in police training. If we train police officers how to perform hands-on tasks while in a classroom, they are likely to recall less of what they learned when they are in the field. We need to do more realistic, context-dependent, hands-on scenario-training that involves stress.

Advice

Train police officers in the environment in which they will be performing their tasks. It may seem trivial, but science suggests the brain ties the lessons to the environment. The more the learning environment mimics the working environment, the stronger the lessons are encoded into memory.

I recall learning many of my active shooter lessons in a classroom. It wasn't very realistic. To improve recall, put police officers in their natural working environment and teach them how to handle realistic situations. The lessons will be more readily recalled when needed most.

Discussions

1. When you were trained in your basic police skills, did your learning environment always mimic the real-world environment you would operate in?

2. Provide some examples where instructors taught basic skills in a context dependent environment that you would consider unique.

3. Share some ideas for how your training programs could be improved by using context dependent learning.

Chapter 6

Improving Learning and Recall

Is there a role for humor while training officers on critical, life-saving, skills?

The flight attendant begins dolling out the obligatory, in fact, federally mandated, pre-flight safety instructions. If you're a frequent flyer, your situational awareness is probably pretty low. You know the routine and it's boring. If you're an infrequent flyer, the monotone, or should I say "mono-drone" voice, of the lead flight attendant is enough to make you bury your eyes deep into the sky magazine. But, on this flight to Vegas, something's different.

The flight attendant begins by saying:

"Our airline employs some of the safest pilots in the industry. Unfortunately, our flight today doesn't have any of them, so you'd better fasten your seat belt and pay close attention to what I'm about to lay down. We're (undisclosed) airlines and we're going to take all your money".

All eyes and ears were immediately fixated on the lead flight attendant. Trust me, I was on the flight and witnessed it first-hand. This was one of the best stand-up comedic routines I've seen in a long time. I actually enjoyed the flight briefing.

Funny Flight Attendant

What made a speech I've heard over 50 times so interesting? There are two explanations, both rooted deep in our cognitive brain. First, the speech was unexpected. We listen with baited anticipation to hear things that surprise us. That's why talk show hosts and newscasters bait listeners with phrases like, "When we come back we're going to show you an amazing video you're not going to want to miss" and we wait to see it.

Second, it was emotional. Emotional messages (and it doesn't matter what emotion the messages invoke) not only capture and keep our attention, but they help in the uptake and storage of those messages into long-term memory. That's right, you tend to remember and recall emotional messages and events with much more accuracy than boring messages and boring events. How well does it work? That flight attendant greeting I shared with you was from a flight I took in 2017, and I remember it like it was yesterday.

Ok…for you instructors out there who are sharing important, life-saving messages – remember, make portions of your message unexpected and use emotions. Both will not only keep attention, but they will also help in learning and recall. Anyone who has attended one of my programs knows I use a healthy dose of both. The results are truly win-win. The attendees are satisfied with their day of learning on how to survive an active shooter event. I have the satisfaction of knowing those lessons are going to stick with the attendees for a long time.

I teach my students that when they go in for a job interview to use appropriate humor or some other tactic to separate themselves from all the other candidates. If they don't, they will be just a number. Use humor and emotional content to help your lessons stick with your audience.

Advice

When doing training try adding emotional and humorous messages. These will help the listeners retain and recall the lessons you teach them. By using emotional and humorous messages, it will break up mundane training and help your audience be more attentive.

Discussions

1. Discuss how to use appropriate humor in your next training lesson.

2. Discuss creative ways to use emotional messages into training scenarios and training lessons.

3. Discuss ways to make mundane trainings more memorable and improve the audience recall of your most important points.

Chapter 7

Freelancing

In some police departments it is standard practice for the first arriving officer on-scene to deploy independently. Oftentimes these officers are highly trained, highly motivated and action oriented. What they are lacking is coordination of their efforts. The potential problem with independent action is it may be unrealistic to think multiple individuals can arrive at varied times and make the same assessment of the situation/conditions and know, automatically, what other officers are doing and the goals they are trying to accomplish. This can cause problems with team and incident situational awareness.

A Play Book

It is important for police officers to have a shared understanding of each member's role during high risk operations. This complicated task may be easier to accomplish when everyone is trained to a common set of procedures. Standard Operating Procedures (SOPs) or Standard Operating Guidelines (SOGs) can help ensure members understand the performance expectations. Unfortunately, some organizations do not have SOPs or SOGs – they have no playbook. A lack of written Standards does not automatically spell trouble for police officers but it is a contributing factor in many casualty investigations.

Rehearsal

As important as having a play book, practicing the plays is equally important. If an organization has written Standards but does not train personnel on how to perform coordinated actions based on the Standards the incident operations are likely to be disjointed and confusing. It cannot be assumed that writing and distributing Standards is going to result in a common understanding of their meaning or a well-coordinated operation.

Coordinated Actions

In addition to having a playbook and practicing, it is important (and sometimes overlooked) that police officers still need to be coordinated. Complex and dynamically changing incidents are commonplace. Incident circumstances often require actions that cannot follow written Standards. The more unique the problem, the greater the likelihood for resilient problem solving. Professional football teams have play books and they practice those plays to perfect their coordination repetitively. Yet teams still have coaches and coordinators to ensure the members perform in a coordinated way.

To ensure team success, be that a sports team or an emergency response team, someone needs to establish and maintain a big picture view of the field/incident right from the beginning and coordinate the actions of all the participants. This is especially important for police officers because the participants almost always arrive in a staggered fashion. This is unlike a sporting event where the team members are all present from the start and it's easier for the coach to coordinate the actions. Absent someone to coordinate actions, an incident can degrade as the independent, uncoordinated actions of police officers fail to achieve a common goal. The situational awareness at an incident is dependent on the coordinated actions of each team member.

Advice

Develop standard operating procedures/guidelines. Practice them as teams, in context to how the team members will perform in realistic environments. Ensure one of the first arriving police officers assumes the role of incident commander and coordinates the activities of other police officers. The person in charge should maintain a "big picture" view of the incident.

As soon as possible, however, someone needs to assume a role as the coordinator of other incoming personnel. This is where the coordinator can pay-off in spades by ensuring all the essential tasks are being assigned and coordinated.

Discussions

1. Discuss the challenges that can arise from engaging in independent actions without coordination.

2. Discuss an incident where independent actions challenged incident coordination and impacted situational awareness of incident personnel.

3. Discuss ideas for how to improve team situational awareness and multiple police officer coordination at dynamically changing incidents.

Chapter 8

Complacency Kills

Curiosity killed the cat, but it's not curiosity that is killing police officers, it's complacency contributing to flawed situational awareness. What does it mean to be complacent? I could offer you the Webster's dictionary definition, instead, I'd like to offer you a definition based on my observations of those who suffer from the affliction.

Complacent

To believe that bad things only happen to other people; To fall into a comfortable rut of apathy – laziness; To have enjoyed success for so long as to believe all actions will result in successful outcomes; To rely on knowledge and skills that have grown stale for lack of practice and renewal; To develop a sense of indifference – to lack concern for – one's safety and well-being. Let's break this down now by expounding on each component of the definition.

In Law Enforcement we are very prone to becoming complacent on the job. As a matter of fact, most police officers die in the middle of their career. According to Kevin Gilmartin, author of Emotional Survival for Law Enforcement, most police officers die feloniously on duty between year 10-15 of their career. Complacency is a big contributing factor to this.

Some of the ways I have shown my complacency on the job have to deal with traffic stops and alarm calls. I remember making traffic stop after traffic stop and using good tactics and nothing ever bad happened. Until one time when I let my guard down and used poor tactics. I stopped an individual and causally walked up to the car thinking to myself this is just another routine traffic stop, when he opened his driver's door, hopped out and started screaming "just kill me." Thankfully, he did not have a weapon on him and I was able to deescalate the situation, but he definitely caught me by surprise and had the tactical advantage on me from my being complacent.

I can also remember going to a lot of alarm calls in my career. 99% of the time the alarm calls were false alarms, were set off by the cleaners, or animals inside of a home tripped the alarm. However, one time I was called to an audible burglar alarm covering glass break. I arrived thinking this would be just another false alarm. To my surprise it wasn't, it was the real deal. Someone had done a smash and grab at one of our local gas stations and took the cash register. Here again I did a poor approach to the building and was being very complacent which could have got me killed.

Believing Bad Things Only Happen to Other People

This is often rooted in a mindset of judgment. While watching a video or reading about a casualty incident, the complacent police officer becomes a judge. The mindset is not one of trying to understand the root cause of what happened and to extract the lessons behind the lessons. Instead, the complacent police officer wants to ridicule and offer judgment upon the misfortunes of others. One who is judging, cannot learn. This causes the lessons to be missed and perpetuates the belief that bad things only happen to other people.

Falling into a Comfortable Rut of Apathy – Laziness

The energy required to develop and maintain competency is immense. It requires both a cognitive and physical effort to develop the knowledge and skills essential for top performance. Any deviation from being exceptionally prepared will result in a consequence, right? Hardly, in fact, the vast majority of cases with large deviations from top performance have no consequence.

That is both a blessing and a curse. If such deviations always resulted in casualties, the results would be catastrophic. For that, we are blessed. Yet it is the same lack of consequence that promotes apathy. The proof that one needs not work as hard, rests in the successful outcomes achieved despite a reduction in knowledge and skill development/maintenance.

Relying on Knowledge and Skills That Have Grown Stale for Lack of Practice and Renewal

For skill and knowledge to be retained and useful, they must be practiced over and over again… and then over and over AGAIN… rinse and repeat. The process of learning and relearning skills is never ending. The pathways that access knowledge in our brains are strengthened through repetition. Just because something was learned in school 10 years ago does not mean the skillset is still flawless. Every expert in every field practices incessantly to keep their skills sharp. So must police officers!

The complacency within an organization is often a byproduct of the organization's culture, undisciplined leadership and individual member mindsets. **This can change**. The journey of one thousand miles begins with a single step. Do something today… take a step toward reducing complacency.

Everyday life

Complacency happens in everyday life all the time. This can be dangerous when working with power tools or using knives in your kitchen. Think of the last time you were operating a chain saw. Did you get complacent as time went on? How about the last time you were slicing up some food. Did you cut yourself because you became complacent? We need to stay focused so we don't become a victim to complacency.

Discussions

1. Discuss what ways you combat complacency.

2. Discuss what training you implement in your department to avoid becoming complacent.

3. Discuss how you can assist your partners if you notice they're becoming complacent.

Chapter 9

Fatigue

Research has shown that fatigue can impact situational awareness in disturbing ways. Some police officers think if they take a "safety nap" it will help. And in a small way, it may help. Any rest is better than no rest. However, a nap does not resolve systemic fatigue. Rest is a critical component to brain function and when there is not adequate rest or disrupted sleep cycles, the impact can be real and measurable.

Some scientists have described the behavior of research participants suffering from fatigue as displaying the same qualities as a person who is intoxicated. When you think about the critical nature of police officer decision making, fatigue can have catastrophic consequences.

The schedules of some police departments are not conducive to adequate rest. I remember working 12-hour shifts from 6 pm - 6 am and then having to be at traffic court by 9 am. Sometimes court would run from 9 am - 12 pm and then I would have to go home, try and get some sleep, and be back for my shift at 6 pm.

This schedule significantly impacted both my mood and my job performance. Other times, I would work 6 pm - 6 am and be informed from a supervisor that a day shifter had called in sick and they needed me to cover the shift until 10 am or noon. This would make for some long hours awake and, thinking back, it severely impacted situational awareness, my decision making, and thus, my safety.

There is a reason truck drivers and airplane pilots are required (by law) to get a certain number of hours of sleep between shifts. Yet, police officers have no such requirement. Police Officers are expected to make high-risk, split-second decisions that could possibly take someone's life and we aren't required to have a certain number of hours of sleep between shifts. I believe this is something we need to work on changing.

Police officers may believe if they feel physically rested, they are not mentally rested. When the body rests, physically, the brain does not rest. In fact, the brain is surprisingly active while the body is resting, suggesting the body rests so the brain may have access to the glucose (energy) to do its heavy lifting. And what is the brain doing while you sleep? The research of neuroscientists tells us our brains are sorting through all the data from our previous waking period, cataloging the events into memory for future use. Hence, fatigue can not only impact short-term performance and memory, it can also impact long-term recall.

Got a perplexing problem? Sleeping on it really does help!

Key Takeaways

Police officers who work long hours should be provided with opportunities to rest their brains. It's not a matter of being lazy as some uninformed people may suggest. It's a matter of personal safety and quality of care to the citizens they serve. Ask yourself who you would want taking care of your community, a well-rested police officer or one that is mentally fatigued?

Everyday Life

Sleep is very important in our lives. Think of the last time you didn't get enough sleep. How did this affect you? Find some time in your busy schedule to wind down and get some rest. Try to avoid watching TV at night and instead read a book or listen to soft music before bedtime.

Remember, the consequences of fatigue impacts you as well as others around you.

Discussions

1. Discuss a time when your situational awareness and decision quality was impacted from being fatigued.

2. Share some ideas about how to obtain adequate rest while working extended shifts.

3. Share some tips for getting adequate rest when off-duty.

Chapter 10

The Silent Killer of Police Officers

My days at the police academy were a lot of fun. I can remember the first day like it was yesterday. We all showed up eager to learn, got our room assignments, did our physical tests and greeted each other in the gymnasium. Most of the cadets knew each other and were from the same school. I was the only one from my school, but it didn't take long to make friends with everyone else.

Our day consisted of learning all the important skills police officers need to know on the job. We spent hours at the gun range, participated in defensive tactics, drove the squad cars like we stole them, pepper sprayed each other, and went through numerous different scenario-type trainings. After the day was done, we made sure to head to the local establishments to have a few adult beverages and share our dreams of where this great law enforcement career would (hopefully) take us.

Looking back, I noticed the instructors did a great job preparing us for the on-duty portion of job and how to maintain officer safety. However, they didn't speak much about how to handle the job, mentally, off-duty and the toll it could take on us. Law enforcement, in particular, is a very high stress job that will expose you to a lot of things most people should never experience. For the longest time, this career had a "tough guy" stigma attached to it. Sharing your thoughts and feelings about calls that you have been on was considered weird and taboo.

The Officer Down Memorial website (https://www.odmp.org/), reveals 62 police officers were killed by felonious assault, gunfire, vehicle pursuit and vehicle assault in 2019. According to B.L.U.E. Help (https://bluehelp.org/) a website that provides statistics on suicides by police officers, 197 police officers took their own life in 2019. That means for every officer feloniously killed in the line of duty approximately three more take their own life by suicide. This is inexcusable. We need to do a better job of taking care of ourselves and our fellow brothers and sisters in blue.

During my tenure, I was lucky enough to participate in a peer support group for first responders. This was a great way to debrief after a call that exposed responders to trauma. I believe these types of programs were setup for the right reasons and encouraged responders to share their feelings and how they were impacted.

According to Mary Wolf, a licensed psychologist, with decades of experience: "It is time to normalize asking for help. Let's make it ok to reach out at the first sign of distress instead of suffering in silence for years. Let's make learning about common reactions and stressors of police work part of training from day one. Let's make emotional health a real priority in an industry that has put it last."

A Call to Action

Let's teach the skills needed to holistically be a police officer: Coping with chronic and acute stress, utilizing exercise as the natural anti-depressant that it is, supporting your colleagues, and asking what you need to effectively do this important work.

Let's talk about the difficulty of domestic violence calls, tragic accidents, and threats to your safety.

Let's make it alright to bring your whole self to the job.

Let's talk openly about what brings out our fears, anger, frustrations and overwhelming sadness in how some people treat their children.

Let's make resources easy to access so everyone knows what to do when a challenge arises whether it's personal or professional.

Let's make it ok to talk about critical incidents and the affects it is having on us.

Let's make it the norm to talk with supervisors, peers, and professionals about how we are feeling and how we are Really doing.

Let's show some vulnerability and humanity in our work.

Trust and connection are key needs in order to sustain a meaningful career. Everyone needs an objective and confidential person that they can confide in, where they can be themselves, and not have to pretend to be happy.

If you are experiencing depression, anxiety, PTSD, addiction, or suicidal thoughts, a licensed mental health professional is your best avenue. You need a mental health provider who understands the unique aspects of police culture. Search for a list of mental health professionals who are covered by your health insurance. Many plans provide mental health counsellors for a small or no co-pay. You might have to make a few calls to find someone who understands the first responder world.

Key Takeaways

Suicide, depression, and other mental health issues are a silent killer among public safety personnel. We need to take better care of ourselves not just physically, but mentally as well. We need to make sure we seek additional support if we are having a hard time in our career fields. If you find you're having disturbing thoughts that won't leave after a high stress call, understand you're having a normal reaction to an abnormal circumstance. We need to make sure we're having a check-up from the neck up.

Everyday Life

Our mental health is extremely important. We need to make sure we have a clear mind and are getting things off our chest. Gone are the days of bottling everything up until they spill over. Find a healthy way to cope with the stresses of the job.
Remember, the consequences of not getting help impacts you as well as others around you.

Discussions

1. Discuss healthy strategies for coping with the stresses of the job.

2. Discuss what plan your agency has to assist public safety personnel having a difficult time dealing with the stresses of the job.

3. Discuss ways your agency could implement a peer support group for your public safety partners, including what training should be provided.

Chapter 11

B.R.E.A.T.H.E.

We know from previous articles that situational awareness is the ability to perceive and understand what is happening around you while being mindful of time passing, and then being able to accurately predict future events in time to avoid bad outcomes.

This is very important when it comes to conflict management and de-escalation as well. As a young police officer I didn't know the proper ways to de-escalate situations and I had very poor situational awareness. I wasn't able to read people's body language and perceive what it was telling me. I often used attack words such as "calm down!" or "come here!" while using my fingers to motion them to walk towards. Unbeknownst to me, this was actually having the reverse effect. I wasn't de-escalating the situation. I was actually escalating the situation.

It took me several years on the job as a patrol officer to recognize people's body language and then to deploy empathy to de-escalate the situation. I learned how to understand what makes people upset during a crisis situation. Often, I was the first face they saw. I don't think they were intentionally displaying anger toward me. They were simply upset and not thinking rationally. Deploying good de-escalation techniques and conflict management skills can save your life.

To help, I developed a process (and an acronym) police officers can use to help gain compliance and maintain good situational awareness. I call it the B-R-E-A-T-H-E technique.

<u>B</u>reathe: Take a couple of slow, deep breaths to relax yourself while using your perception skills. Breathing can help calm you down and allow you to think rationally and rational thinking is critical to good decision making. What is the person you're dealing with telling you, both verbally and non-verbally?

Controlled breathing can help reduce the undesirable effects of stress (e.g., tunnel vision) and relax your mind to think logically.

Recognize: Be vigilant of what's happening around you while being mindful of how time is passing. What's being discussed? Have you seen this situation before? For example, does the suspect you're dealing with have his/her hands in their pockets and won't take them out? Is your red flag warning sign going off? By recognizing a situation like this, you can keep yourself safe and rely on training. By recognizing the danger signs (clues and cues) you're displaying good situational awareness.

Examine: Is this an emotional situation or logical situation? Is this person you're trying to de-escalate in a logical state of mind or are they highly emotional and possibly in a crisis situation? I can remember some people coming into our lobby of the police department very agitated because they just received a parking ticket. I examined them and determined they were in an emotional charged state and not thinking logically. It's a good idea to empathize with people in this situation and repeat back to them what they're saying by using good active listening skills. Empathy can calm the emotions.

Abstain: Restrain yourself from engaging in conflict or from making a quick, irrational decision. Again, take your time and don't rush the situation. Like most problems to be solved, slowing the pace and allowing some time for emotions to settle down usually leads to better decisions and better outcomes.

Think: Think of your course of action. Restrain yourself from engaging in conflict or a quick irrational decision. This is very tough to do. Like many officers, I have struggled to restrain myself many of times. And when I failed to properly restrain myself, it usually led to a physical confrontation, which could have resulted in me getting hurt or becoming the subject of legal action.

Stressed brains revert to basic human instinct, of which the foundation is survival. This can trigger an automatic fight or flight response.

When an officer is under severe stress and the fight or flight kicks in, the officer no longer has conscious control over their response. And this is where things can go wrong quickly. Take a second to breathe and try your best to not let the person you're dealing with trigger your emotions. They are behaving emotionally and having an emotional response. You're the one that needs to have a calming presence and be the voice of reason. Think ahead of the situation and predict where it could go and how you can prevent a bad outcome.

<u>H</u>andle: Take care of the situation in a calm and professional manner. As police officers, we are trusted by the public to display a calming presence. We must show we can handle the situation professionally. If we don't, the situation can spin out of control quickly and use of force may escalate. Under extreme stress, we can experience multiple barriers that can impact situational awareness and performance, including tunnel vision (narrowing of our visual field), auditory exclusion (going deaf) and loss of fine motor skills. We will perform best when we remain calm. We can practice controlling our stress by practicing de-escalation techniques during realistic scenario-based training.

<u>E</u>xamine: After an encounter, ask yourself what went well? How can you perform better in the future? Debriefing is so important in everything we do. We will be well-served to identify opportunities where we can improve our conflict management and de-escalation skills. As police officers we know that every call is different. With experience we become better at reading people and improve our situational awareness skills over time. Building scenario-based verbal de-escalation training into your annual use of force training can be very beneficial.

Everyday Life

De-escalation is very important in everyday life. Whether we're talking with our co-workers, a significant other, or our kids, good de-escalation techniques are extremely valuable.

Learn how to recognize when someone is in a highly emotional state and not thinking rationally. Good de-escalation techniques can help save relationships and prevent destroying friendships and marriages.

The next time you see someone in a highly emotional state and not thinking rationally don't tell them to CALM DOWN! This never works. Instead use good active listening skills and say something like: "I just want to make sure I'm hearing you correctly. Is this what you're telling me (fill in the blank)." This shows you're using good active listening skills and you're repeating back what the person has said.

Discussions

1. Share some examples where you have used de-escalation and conflict management skills.

2. Discuss training your department has in place to incorporate de-escalation and conflict management strategies.

3. Discuss how you can assist your partners if you notice they are struggling with these techniques.

Chapter 12

Meta Awareness

Developing and maintaining situational awareness at an emergency scene can be a very challenging task. Scenes are often stressful, complex, time-compressed, and complicated with rapidly-changing conditions. Police officers have lots of information to process and many tasks to perform. And, sadly, situational awareness isn't always front-of-mind. Under such conditions, meta awareness may help.

Awareness About Awareness

Meta awareness is a term we derived from the work of developmental psychologist, John Flavell, who coined the term "metacognition" to describe a phenomenon where a person has cognition about cognition or, stated another way, they are thinking about what they are thinking about. Applied to situational awareness, the term "meta awareness" would mean you are actually (in a conscious state) thinking about your situational awareness.

As noted previously, it may not be intuitive (or automatic) for police officers to be consciously thinking about their situational awareness while fulfilling all their duties and responsibilities during an emergency response. If an officer is able to elevate awareness to the conscious level, then it (awareness) becomes as important in the mind of the officer as anything else they may be doing or thinking about.

How to Use Meta Awareness

Before we go down the path of how to develop meta awareness, it may be appropriate to offer a working definition of situational awareness.

Situational awareness is:

> An individual's ability to **perceive** information (clues and cues) about what is happening in his or her environment and to **understand** the meaning of those clues and cues (in the context of how time is passing). And then, be able to make accurate **predictions**
> about future events (in time to avoid bad outcomes).

Meta awareness is a purposeful focus (at a conscious level) of how you are developing and maintaining your situational awareness. One way you can accomplish this is by employing "self-speak".

Intrapersonal Communications

Do you ever talk to yourself? Of course you do. We all do. This internal, personal dialog is known as intrapersonal communications or "self-speak". Self-help gurus teach their clients to use positive self-speak to maintain a conscious awareness of what is important or what to focus on in order to accomplish goals. The same concept can be applied in the formation and maintenance of situational awareness.

An Example

Here's an example of how meta awareness can help in forming and maintaining situational awareness. The scenario I will use is a police officer in a high speed pursuit. I will play the role of the police officer and share how I would deploy self-speak:

Ok, Drew. Remember your acronym B-R-E-A-T-H-E take a breath to keep calm (breathe in for 4 seconds, hold for 4 seconds, out for 4 seconds, pause for 4 seconds).

*My situational awareness starts with **perception**. I must conduct a size-up to gather factual information about what is happening. In my 360-degree size-up I am going to use my eyes and ears to gather clues and cues. The most important pieces of information I need to gather include:*

1. ***What crime was just committed?*** – *Was this a crime of violence? Or just a simple property crime in which a vehicle was stolen?*

2. ***Environment*** – *Is it nighttime or daytime? What's my backdrop look like if I have to shoot? What are traffic conditions?*

3. ***Can I use a PIT maneuver*** – *Does the crime warrant a PIT maneuver? What does my policy state? Can I ram the vehicle?*

4. ***Speed*** – *How fast are we traveling? Are other agencies putting out spike strips? How fast are conditions changing?*

5. ***Policy*** – *Is there a supervisor on that can shut this pursuit down? Am I the senior officer on and have to make the call? What does my policy state?*

6. ***Resources*** – *What is the quality and quantity of resources I have available to me at this moment in time? Are there other agencies that can assist or am I solo? I need to use this information to form my **understanding** of what is happening to help me make an action plan. (pause and think).*

Now it's time to make some decisions:

Critical Decision #1: Should I PIT the vehicle? If I have another agency with me this might be the best situation as quickly as possible.

Critical Decision #2: Should I follow for a while to look for the best place to stop this vehicle?

*Critical Decision #3: Do I disengage? If so, I need to completely stay out of the pursuit and listen to my supervisor and announce on the radio I have terminated. Now it's time to **predict** future outcomes:*

Benchmark: What do I expect to be the outcome of my action plan?

Deadline: What is a reasonable deadline to accomplish this benchmark? (With consideration to #1-6 above.)

How much time should it take for the benchmark to be achieved? (The answer to this takes into consideration the critical factors mentioned above: Crime, Environment, Speed, PIT, Policy, Resources).

Only after I have completed this process will I take an action. While it seems like it would take a long time to work through this process, it really doesn't. This can be accomplished in 1-2 minutes, depending on how long it takes to complete the size-up. Of course, the more you practice this process, the better (and faster) you'll be at completing it.

Advice

There are many barriers that will try to impact your ability to form and maintain situational awareness – pre-arrival lens, task fixation, mission myopia, stress, urgency, culture, and peer-pressure (to name a few). There are multiple stimuli competing for your attention as well – your partner/other officers looking for orders, radio traffic to be answered, civilian issues to be addressed, etc.

On top of all of this, there is a high speed pursuit happening – saving lives and property and ensuring officer and citizen safety. With consideration for the complexity of an emergency scene, it can be easy to lose track of critical information and it can be easy to forget just how important developing and maintaining your situational awareness is.

Talk to yourself and use meta awareness to help you develop and maintain your situational awareness. Of course, it's also a great idea to talk with fellow officers about the same criteria. This helps ensure the team is on the same page.

Discussions

1. Discuss how police officers can use intrapersonal communications to help form and maintain situational awareness.

2. Practice using self-talk (out loud) during training sessions.

3. Make a habit of asking fellow officers: "What's on your mind?" as a way to encourage them to share their self-speak.

Chapter 13

Hyper Vigilance

Hyper vigilance is a biological response to stress that causes your senses to go on high alert for danger. Your body goes on super alert status because it senses there is danger in the area. The hormones trigger biological changes that increase the acuity of your senses.

Stated another way, hyper vigilance can help your eyes see things that they might not have otherwise seen if you were not under stress. Likewise, hyper vigilance can help your ears hear things that they might not have otherwise heard if you were not under stress.

And, for the sake of avoiding the annoyance of being repetitive, suffice it to say that all your senses are equally hyper aroused and on high alert. The stress of an emergency scene leads your brain to think there is danger in the area which makes your thinking (and in some cases your actions) primal.

Primal Goal #1: Survive!

The goal of the body and brain in a stress-induced, hyper aroused state is simple, Survive! What is out there that can kill you? Can you kill it? Can you outrun it? Those are the questions your brain is grappling with and your alert senses will help it make that determination. The human body is well-suited (based on genetic adaptation) to deal with these short-term stressors.

It was that kind of stress your cave-dwelling ancestors dealt with every day. Eat or be eaten. It was a pretty simple existence out there on the Serengeti. There were no worries about 401k plans, bad economies, looming mortgage payments or kids not doing well in school. The stresses of your daily lives are very different and in many ways – far more chronic and for more cumulative. On the upside, you don't have to worry about a T-rex eating your kids when they leave the house.

So, we've established it. Hyper vigilance is a good thing! Well, don't pop the Champagne corks yet. We're not done.

The downside of hyper vigilance

Your brain is a wonderment of science, that is for certain. It can do things that no computer can duplicate. But it does have some limitations. One of those limitations is how much information it can take in, process, comprehend and recall at any one time. The question of just how much information that is intrigued the research community and in 1956 a cognitive psychologist at Princeton University named George Miller provided the shocking answer.

Seven! The average person can hold about seven pieces of unrelated information in their working (short term) memory, give or take two (for those slightly above and slightly below average performers). Miller's studies have been robustly confirmed in numerous studies since. Coincidentally, it was the results of Miller's research that led to the original seven-digit telephone numbering system in the United States.

This is where hyper vigilance can turn ugly in a hurry. Because your senses are hyper aroused, they are taking in more information about your surroundings. If your surroundings are simple and basic (like fighting a saber-toothed tiger in the jungle of the East Savannah (as your cave-dwelling ancestors did), then you didn't have to worry about your brain getting overwhelmed with information.

But, put that brain on an emergency scene with dozens, maybe even hundreds of pieces of data coming at you and you are on the fast-track for overload. Some of the data is in writing, some audible, most is visual and nearly all of it is changing rapidly. It is easy to get overwhelmed in a hurry.

Advice

The solution to this problem was uncovered during the research conducted by cognitive psychologist Gary Klein, also known for his discovery of the Recognition-Primed Decision Making Process.

Klein's research involved trying to understand the decision making processes used by public safety commanders. One of the questions to be answered was: How do you make sense of it all? How do you process and comprehend so many clues and cues?

The answer was a stunner and entirely unexpected. The expert-level public safety commanders said they don't try to process and comprehend all the information. In fact, there is just a small number of critical pieces of information essential for making a good decision. Commanders noted if they tried to comprehend it all, it would be impossible.

So, what should be on the short list for critical information to capture and process? Obviously, the answer would vary for each type of emergency you deal with.

The take-away lesson is: Stress causes hyper vigilance which increases your acuity. In a complex, fast-paced environment, that can accelerate cognitive overload. Less information, so long as it's the right information, is your best ally. There are a couple more caveats about the information. The more complex the information, the more likely you are to be overwhelmed. The more detailed the information is, the more likely you are to be confused. And the more unfamiliar the information is, the more time you will need because you have to learn what the information means.

Discussions

1. Pick a type of emergency and detail the 7 (or less) critical pieces of information you think are essential to making a good decision.

2. What tricks and secrets do you have for managing information in complex environments?

3. Describe a situation where you realized, maybe even after the fact, that your senses were hyper vigilant and you heard or saw things that you might not have otherwise seen or heard.

Chapter 14

Frustration Can Impact Situational Awareness

Anyone who's been frustrated knows it can consume a lot of your mental energy and thinking space. This can significantly impact your situational awareness. In fact, depending on the level of frustration, your brain can be hijacked by all-consuming thoughts about what is causing the angst. While operating at an emergency scene, frustration may draw your attention away from perceiving and understanding critical clues and cues that form situational awareness.

Some sources of frustration

There are many things that can cause frustration at an emergency scene. As I reflect back on my experience and conversations with police officers, I can offer this small list of sources of frustrations that can impact your situational awareness:

1. Receiving incomplete or inaccurate information from dispatch about the nature or details of the emergency you are responding to.

2. Delayed response times because of a train or traffic jam.

3. Fellow police officers that did not know how to perform their jobs effectively (this includes not only technical job knowledge but also being physically unfit to perform the duties, causing a team member to fatigue quickly).

4. Tasks not being completed as quickly as you expected your fellow police officers to complete the tasks, or tasks not being completed at all.

5. Performing independent actions (i.e., freelancing). Police officers performing actions that are not consistent with the overall incident objectives, causing confusion and safety concerns.

6. Police officers complaining about having to do their jobs, sitting on calls too long, or dodging calls.

7. Inadequate equipment to get the task done efficiently or general lack of equipment or other resources.

With little effort, I am confident you could easily add to the list of things that have frustrated you from time to time while operating at incident scenes. And, if you're being honest, you'd probably admit that your mind wasn't completely on-task while you were preoccupied with the frustrating issue or condition.

Tangible example

I can recall a good example of being frustrated when I was dispatched to a motorist assist in my city. While enroute to the call my partner was dispatched to a property damage accident on the highway. My partner got on the radio and said he was very close to my motorist assist and requested that we change calls. I agreed with him, and we advised dispatch we would change calls.

I found out later that my partner had driven past his property damage accident, and it had multiple vehicles involved and included some commercial vehicles. It was a huge mess! I was so frustrated by my partner that I became very angry on my call and didn't treat the people I was dealing with very well. I noticed my attention being drawn away from other critical tasks.

Advice

It can be very difficult to control your frustration at an incident scene, especially when expectations are not being met. If you find yourself becoming frustrated, and thus fixated on something happening, try these suggestions:

1. Be mindful at all times of the role you are playing and how important it is for you to stay focused on your role for your safety and the safety of others.

2. If the source of frustration can be set aside and dealt with later, delay addressing it at the incident scene. Of course, matters of safety should be addressed immediately to prevent harm to members and civilians.

3. Employ a stress reduction breathing technique: Breathe in on a four-count. Hold for a four-count. Breathe out on a four-count. Delay your next inhalation for a four-count. This will cause a small increase in carbon dioxide levels in the blood and slow the release of chemicals that can hyper-focus attention. The old adage of "take a deep breath" has some merit.

4. If you are in the command role, consider delegating the frustrating issue to a subordinate and let them resolve it. This will allow you to keep your focus on the important task of commanding the big-picture incident.

5. If you must address the source of frustration, be courteous and professional and adopt a mindset of being helpful. Avoid confrontational language or demeanor (like using your frustrated, annoyed or agitated voice).

There is too much at stake if your situational awareness erodes as a result of frustration. And if your eroded situational awareness results in a casualty, you'll be very disappointed in yourself that you yielded your awareness of your critical role to your frustration.

Discussions

1. Discuss a time when your awareness was drawn off-task by a frustration.

2. Discuss some strategies you have used to reduce the impact of frustration.

3. Discuss strategies for addressing frustrating issues in ways that will not make matters worse.

4. Seek out that person who always seems to be calm under pressure and ask them to share their best practices with you.

Chapter 15

Assuming or Creating Risk?

'We will risk a lot to save a lot and risk little to save little.'

There are several variations on this saying, including: 'Great risks will be taken to save savable lives; Moderate risks will be taken to save savable property; and, No risk will be taken to save what is unsavable.' Risk management is an essential component to the development and maintenance of strong situational awareness. I believe these sayings relate to public safety and other high-risk environments. By its nature, public safety is risky and no catchy phrase is going to make it safer. But there is a huge difference between assuming the risk and creating the risk.

First, let me say I am completely guilty of confusing assumed risk and created risk. Here my story:

One afternoon I was working patrol when I heard over the radio a neighboring agency was in pursuit of a motorcycle that had just passed a bunch of cars on the shoulder. The motorcycle was headed toward our city, and I advised I would assist in the pursuit. I saw the neighboring agency officer going at a high rate of speed following a high-performance motorcycle. I swung in behind them and called out that I would be involved in the pursuit and I would call the pursuit on the radio.

Before long I noticed I was way behind my fellow officer and he was taking huge risks that I was not comfortable with (i.e., Heading into oncoming traffic blindly at excessive speeds). The motorcycle eventually crashed (and the driver survived). No officers were hurt in the pursuit. After watching my squad video and debriefing with one of my supervisors I realized that I had created risk in this event and I should have discontinued due to the safety of the public.

I am not judging the officer from the neighboring agency. There are plenty of critics out there who rant from their high perches of judgment, often in non-productive and disrespectful ways.

Tuck this lesson away and recall it often: When we're judging, we cannot be learning. I hope those who read this here will learn and not pass judgment.

Let's apply the maxim: We will risk a lot to save a lot. Will the risk of pursuing this motorcycle be rewarded with a worthwhile outcome?

Police work is risky, in fact, life in general can be risky. Every police officer knows that. But there is a big difference between assuming the risk and creating the risk by performing tasks in ways that are unsafe or inconsistent with best practices and sometimes we hide behind the testosterone-laden mantra, "We're cops. That's what we do!"

I am a police officer with 15+ years of experience. But I also have other obligations (roles) that are important to me. I am a husband, a son, and a brother (both in the biblical and fraternal sense). Maybe I am a selfish person, but as I age, I look at the big picture and analyze if I am creating risk or if the call I'm going on is assumed risk. If I am creating risk, it's not worth it.

It takes a real hero to stand up for safety, especially if surrounded by others who are consumed by their self-anointed hero status.

Advice

1. Acknowledge the risks inherent in the work we do.

2. Learn everything possible about how people get hurt and killed by reading near-miss and line-of-duty death reports.

3. Discuss how to manage risk by using best practices.

4. Ensure the risks being taken are worth the potential reward.

5. Train on SOMETHING every day. The way to ensure peak performance is to make incremental improvements over time.

6. Learn from the outcomes. Even when the outcomes are good, ask, "Did our actions make sense? What were the potential risks? What was the reward we were trying to accomplish?

Discussions

1. Describe what your department does to support taking appropriate risks based on rewards.

2. If your department had a similar experience (e.g., members were creating risk by performing tasks that do not match the conditions) how would you learn from it?

3. Have you ever found yourself performing tasks that did not justify the risk? Did you stop or did you continue?

Chapter 16

Distractions and Interruptions

As I talk with my students in classes about the impact of distractions and interruptions on situational awareness, I find myself often being asked, "What's the difference?" While there are distinctly different causes for distractions and interruptions, the outcome is often very similar…a reduction in situational awareness and the potential for a catastrophic outcome.

A distraction is something that draws one's attention away from what they are supposed to be paying attention to, entirely unintentionally. For example, a police officer working at a scene might be distracted by a loud noise (e.g., an air horn, siren, a scream, or an explosion). This draws the officer's attention to the source of the noise (though it doesn't have to be a noise… it could just as easily be something visual or a smell). While the officer's attention is focused on the sources of the distraction, however brief, their attention is drawn away from what they were giving attention to just prior to the distraction.

An interruption is something that draws one's attention away from what they are supposed to be paying attention to, entirely on purpose. For example, an officer working at a scene might be interrupted by someone talking to them, by being called on the radio or by receiving a cell phone call. The interruption draws the attention of the officer away. However brief, attention is refocused on something new.

The reason distractions and interruptions are so dangerous for police officers are multiple fold. First, emergency scenes are fertile ground for distractions and interruptions. There are often loud noises, bright lights, and lots of things to stimulate the visual and audible senses.

Second, responders like to share information, and this is often done by radio or face-to-face communications. Each interaction is, without passing judgment on how important it may be, an interruption to the receiver's thought process.

Every time a thought is disrupted by a distraction or interruption, the brain leaves one thought behind to pick up on the new one. When this happens, situational awareness is at risk because the return to the original thought may not be to the exact place where the thought was left. Or, even more dangerous, it's possible the brain may never come back to the original thought at all, even though that original thought may have involved the performance of a critical safety task.

Advice

The best way to avoid the impact of distractions and interruptions is to reduce exposure to them. If commanding this incident, this can be accomplished by being physically remote from direct contact to those stimuli that distract and interrupt. This may mean commanding from a short distance away from the action or commanding from within a vehicle. Designate someone to answer phone calls for you if involved in a major critical incident.

Remember a radio transmission is an interruption. Try to avoid having the entire department drawn off task to listen to a radio transmission that may not even pertain to their assignment. And while consideration needs to be given to avoiding tunneled senses it is important to stay focused on the task. Teach your new rookie police officers and staff to only use the radio when necessary. This will avoid numerous distractions and interruptions.

Discussions

1. Describe an incident scene where a distraction impacted your ability to stay focused on your task.

2. Describe an incident scene where an interruption impacted your ability to stay focused on your task.

3. What are some tips and tricks you use to control distractions and interruptions while operating on stimulus-rich emergency scenes?

4. Are your supervisors located remotely or in the thick of the action? What have you observed about their ability to maintain situational awareness based on where they are located?

Chapter 17

Stop Judging to Improve Situational Awareness

Oftentimes when I am talking with police officers about the role of situational awareness and casualty incidents, especially the ones that have recently occurred, they share with me their opinions and frustrations about the performance of the police officers and the decisions made by command staff. If I have learned anything, it's that police officers are very opinionated and, in general, are not very understanding or forgiving when assessing errors of their peers.

Stated another way: Police officers are quick to judge. I used to be this way also. Earlier in my career I would ask: Why were they doing that? Now, I ask: Why did it make sense TO THEM to be doing what they were doing at that moment in time? Asking the latter question opens my mind up to learning. You see, I can offer all kinds of opinions as to why I think the police officers were doing what they were doing. But I cannot possibly know the answer to the latter question without asking the people directly involved.

It is critical to learn everything possible about why casualty events occur so the lessons can improve the safety of all police officers. My students often look at a police videos and make a quick judgement about what they see. I tell them we need to take a moment and understand the officer's point of view. We have to factor in that we're using hindsight to judge their actions. An officer has a split second to respond to a rapidly evolving event. They have to make a decision that they will live with forever. After the event, observers and critics have all the time in the world to judge their actions.

Recently, I asked my students if it's ever acceptable to shoot a suspect 17 times? Most of my students said absolutely not and that would be excessive force. I then played them a video out of Chicago where it showed an individual not listening to police officers. He had a large knife and charged at a female officer. She tried tasing him twice with no success.

The other two police officers had to shoot this man 17 times before he fell. Even after that, he was still clinching onto the female officer he was trying to stab. I believe I proved my point and the students understood.

Unfortunately, in society today there are many people who want to judge the work of police officers. These critics have never worn our uniform or even done a ride-along. Their perspective is from the outside and they have never had to make the decisions police officers are faced with every day. I believe this quote by Theodore Roosevelt sums it up the best:

> *"It is not the critic who counts; not the man who points out how the strong man stumbles, or where the doer of deeds could have done them better. The credit belongs to the man who is actually in the arena, whose face is marred by dust and sweat and blood; who strives valiantly; who errs, who comes short again and again, because there is no effort without error and shortcoming; but who does actually strive to do the deeds; who knows great enthusiasms, the great devotions; who spends himself in a worthy cause; who at the best knows in the end the triumph of high achievement, and who at the worst, if he fails, at least fails while daring greatly, so that his place shall never be with those cold and timid souls who neither know victory nor defeat."*

Advice

When police officers stop judging and start learning, situational awareness will improve. Borrowing from Steven Covey's Seven Habits of Highly Effective People: "Seek first to understand, then to be understood." Stop judging the performance of fellow officers and seek to understand why the actions and decision they made, at the time of the casualty event, made sense to the them.

Everyday Life

Judging is so easy to do. We can sit back and judge nearly every incident out there. However, are we just a critic? Or are we the person in the arena? Have some respect when you hear headlines of a bad action done by an officer. Pay close attention to the factors that led to this incident happening. Don't be so quick to judge. Think of what the officer perceived and understood at the time of the incident.

Discussions

1. Discuss the process your department uses to learn from your near-miss and bad incidents.

2. Discuss the process you use to learn from the near-miss and bad incidents that occur in other departments.

3. Discuss the value of having a facilitated debriefing (conducted by an independent facilitator) to help your organization learn from near-miss and casualty events.

Chapter 18

When Budgets Impact Staffing

Throughout the police service there are departments whose staffing has been reduced as a result of budget cuts, retirements, and lack of people wanting to get into the field. That is not going to come as a shock to many. What has been shocking for me, however, has been the response to my question of what police department leaders are doing to ensure the situational awareness and safety of line personnel as a result of these cutbacks.

I have heard many, many stories from police leaders about staffing cuts. And when I do, I frequently inquire about how tactics have changed as a result of staffing reductions. It is both shocking and disappointing to get the deer in the headlights look from so many of these leaders. The command staff in many police departments have not held meetings with personnel to discuss how tactics will change as a result of having less personnel. How can we avoid the "deer in the headlights" look?

I can remember back to a time when I worked at my previous department when our minimums were 3 officers per shift. However, on training days and range days the minimum was dropped to 2 officers per shift. I recall one frustrated officer asking at a department meeting, "What's the point of minimum staffing?" The captain's response was, "For your safety." What I found interesting about this was minimums were for our safety but on training days it was ok to dip below minimums so that the department did not have to pay overtime. Thankfully, the administration saw this flaw in the system and corrected it immediately.

When police officers are asked what they're supposed to do differently as a result of reduced staffing I get the same deer in the headlights look. They have no idea. In fact, most of the time the response is, "It's business as usual." But it's not.

If less personnel are responding or if the response times of personnel are going to be delayed then, tactically, the same amount of work cannot get done in the same amount of time and this can compromise police officer safety.

Command's Obligation

Police officers need to hear from command staff, in advance of an emergency, that the game plan is going to change, and the new plan of attack should be shared. Otherwise, police officers will continue to do the same thing they've always done, only with less resources... and greater risk. A competent leader should never let this happen.

Advice

If staffing levels have been reduced or are anticipated to be reduced, command staff should meet with patrol personnel and run through scenarios of how strategies and tactics will change on scenes. A good way to do this is to run a scenario with the former staffing levels, detailing what patrol officers do and what the anticipated outcomes are.

Then run the same scenario with reduced staffing and discuss how the workload and stress changes and how the time to task completion changes.

Discussions

1. If your department has experienced a reduction in staffing, how have your tactics changed to reflect the reduction and to ensure police officer safety?

2. Have your command staff sat down with patrol officers during roll call and lead meaningful discussions about how staffing impacts strategy and tactics and how they plan to change their approach to calls for service?

3. What emergency response challenges from staffing reductions cause you the greatest concerns?

Chapter 19

Active Shooter: Police Officer Response

My students often ask me: "Mr. Moldenhauer, what's the worst call cops could ever go on?" My response is always the same, an active shooter call. I have had my share of terrible calls in my career that will stay with me forever (i.e. suicides, child deaths, and fatal car accidents just to name a few). However, I don't feel any of these could ever be as bad as responding to an active shooter call.

I couldn't imagine the horror of showing up to a call that someone is actively killing innocent people. We in law enforcement all took an oath to protect and serve. The trainings I have been to with my fellow brothers and sisters in blue makes me confident that we will do whatever we can to stop these horrible incidents as fast as humanely possible.

We have come a long way in training for these incidents. I can remember when I first started as a police officer attending active shooter training, we had one goal in mind. That goal was to take out the shooter as fast as possible. While at training we would work on tactical and rapid response techniques on how to stop these violent suspects from killing innocent people.

Taking out the shooter is still our number one priority. However, what do we do with the people that have been shot and are possibly dying? We didn't train on how to save these people when I first started. But now we have improved our training and adopted a new philosophy: STOP THE KILLING, STOP PEOPLE FROM DYING, GET THE INJURED TO A MEDICAL FACILITY. We do this collaboratively with firefighters and EMS.

As police officers we must STOP THE KILLING. After all, we are the ones with the guns and body armor. We need to respond quickly. This was tough for us at first because we were taught that we may need to sacrifice our own safety to stop the killing. When we would attempt to seek cover or use slower, more controlled tactics, our instructors would reprimand us and tell us to keep moving.

They reminded us that every time we heard a gunshot, we were to presume someone was just killed. Our instructors told us the priority of life goes as follows: lives of hostages, lives of innocent civilians, our own life, and lastly the killer's life. This was tough for us to get used to. Throughout the entire police academy and our careers, we were told officer safety is first priority. However, in an active shooter incident, all bets are off and we may need to sacrifice our safety to persevere life.

After the killer has been taken out or contained, we must STOP PEOPLE FROM DYING. We do this by applying tourniquets on people and triaging severe injuries as quick as possible. Several trainings I have been in lately have included assistance from firefighters and EMS personnel. We form teams of firefighters and EMS personnel, protected by police officers, to assist in getting the most severely injured victims out as quick as possible.

I am happy we have incorporated firefighters and EMS personnel into our training. I commend them for their bravery to enter these violent scenes with us. Working together has produced some impressive results. Our final priority is to GET THE INJURED TO A MEDICAL FACILITY. Once the victims are outside the hazard zone, fire and EMS have the primary responsibility for triaging, treating and transporting.

Something to keep in mind with training for active shooter incidents with your department is to keep the training as real as possible. When we train in controlled environments, where we can slowly go through our tactical evolutions, results are near perfect. However, the minute we introduce stress into the scenarios, police officer behavior changes and it impacts our performance.

For example, we may introduce stress by arming the shooter and officers with simulated ammunition (i.e., paintballs) and crank up scary music with screaming and gunshots. This changes everything! Armed with simulated ammunition, I have witnessed police officers, put under stress, shoot other police officers when they round corners, police officers shoot other police officers in the back, officers freeze in doorways and I have witnessed a complete breakdown of communications among teams.

You may recall from my previous article titled "Do We Train to Fail", I noted practice makes permanent. When we respond to one of these horrific calls we must be prepared to handle the extreme stress we are going to encounter. Training that requires officers to perform under highly stressful conditions will improve critical thinking skills and tactical performance.

Key Takeaways

Situational awareness is key to officer survival and will help us save as many lives as possible when dealing with an active shooter. Consider conducting mental rehearsals of active shooter scenarios. During a mental rehearsal you would image yourself in an active shooter situation and think through what the environment would be like. Imagine using all of your senses (e.g., what would you be seeing, hearing, feeling, tasting and smelling). Vividly imagine the situation in as much detail as you can.

Practice "if-then" decision scenarios. For example, you might think: If I was in a hallway and I heard a gunshot on the floor above me, then I would _____ (fill in the blank). Rehearse as many "if-then" scenarios as you could imagine, building complexity into the scenarios as you gain confidence.

One of the benefits of mental rehearsals is two-fold. First, mental rehearsals can reduce surprises. Our critical thinking skills can be impacted by the element of surprise. When you find yourself in a real-world situation that you've mentally rehearsed, you won't be surprised. You'll be expecting it and you will have already thought through one (or more) decision options.

The second advantage of mental rehearsals is they will help improve our prediction skills. In active shooter situations, we have to always be thinking ahead of our current action – being mindful of not only what is happening right now, but also thinking about what is going to happen next (e.g., What's going happen around the next corner?). When practicing "if-then" scenarios and performing mental rehearsals, think beyond yourself. Imagine the actions of other members of your team (e.g., other officers, fire, and EMS personnel who may be with you).

Discussions

1. Discuss how active shooter training under stress changes officer behavior.

2. Discuss the benefits and challenges you can anticipate from working collaboratively with your local fire departments and EMS provider.

3. Share some examples of mental rehearsals you have performed.

4. Share some of the specific "if-then" scenarios you have practiced.

Chapter 20

Active Shooter: Collaborating With Fire And EMS

When I was in the police academy and went through Active Shooter training it was designed solely for police officers. There was never a mention of EMS or fire department response and how they could assist in these situations. It took approximately 8 years into my career until I went to a training that involved the assistance of EMS and firefighters. It really opened my eyes as to how much value EMS and firefighters can add to these catastrophic events.

In the most recent trainings I have participated in, we have incorporated using EMS and firefighters to assist with rapidly evacuating people that have been injured and it significantly improved our efficiency. We set up a rescue team where police officers provide protection and guided a group of EMS and fire personnel through a building to get the injured victims out. Training as a single unit in these rescue teams and working in collaboration with each other has been very beneficial will save more lives.

One of the things I noticed that firefighters do well is they are very good at setting up incident command and being able to communicate well with each other on the radio. Ever since I have been a police officer I have always been really impressed with how fast firefighters mobilize incident command and run their incidents so efficiently.

As police officers this is something we can definitely learn from our partners in the fire service. This works well when an Active Shooter event is unfolding, and teams need to be organized before heading to the hot zone. Firefighters have a lot of experience in incident command and it definitely shows during these collaborative training events.

Words of Advice to Survive an Active Shooter

Active Shooter events are becoming more and more common throughout the United States. It's a good thing to reach out to your fellow agencies to conduct joint training so that everyone is on the same page if one of these events were to ever unfold in your jurisdiction.

It requires coordinating a lot of moving parts and when we train together in a stressful environment we will be better prepared for when real event occurs.

If you're a firefighter or EMS worker and you find yourself on a routine call that rapidly becomes an active shooter event there are a few things you should know and practice. First, if you can safely do so, RUN! Get out of the situation as fast as possible. You'll improve your chances of knowing where to run if, in advance, you are thinking about your way out far before you have to flee (think pre-plan). Once the event turns hostile, you will have little time to think about your escape route.

If running is not a safe option because the shooter too close then you should hide. I'm not talking about hiding under a desk. That, in fact, may be your worst option. Hiding under a desk makes you a sitting duck. Hiding under desks may work in the movies, but it's a bad plan in real life. When I say hide I mean actively barricading behind cover. If you cannot find cover, then find a way to conceal yourself.

Think of cover as a barrier that can stop bullets (e.g., the engine block of a car or a brick wall). Concealment, on the other hand, is something that will conceal (i.e., hide) your body, but bullets can still penetrate through (e.g., drywall or a wood door). When you hide, barricade and lock the door if possible. Put large heavy objects such as tables, computers, or desks in front of the door so it cannot easily be opened. Wait there as long as you need until law enforcement arrives and the officers retrieve you.

Lastly (and only if the first two options don't work) you will need to fight. As a firefighter or EMS worker you can improvise weapons (e.g., SCBA, oxygen tanks, fire extinguishers, scissors). If you are by yourself, your best option is to hurl any object available to you at the shooter and try to get away to cover or run out of the building. Use any means you can imagine to slow down the shooter.

If you are with a group, your best chance of survival is to improvise weapons and throw them all at the shooter all at the same time. Once you are able to distract or confuse the shooter, try to incapacitate the shooter until law enforcement arrives. Think of Flight 93, the group of passengers on that plane used improvised weapons (e.g., hot coffee, carts) and subdued a group of armed terrorists. A group effort is the way to go, it requires training and leadership but will give you the best chances of survival. Keep in mind that acting aggressively toward the shooter is your last resort option.

Do's and Don'ts of Responding to an Active Shooter

I always knew when I arrived on a house fire or accident scene that this is the fire department's jurisdiction. I also knew that when I arrived on a medical scene it belonged to EMS and I was there to provide support. For my fellow brothers and sisters in fire and EMS I have a question for you: Does it frustrate you when a police officer parks in front of a working house fire? How about when a police car blocks your access where someone was having a heart attack and you can't back your ambulance into the driveway?

I would be lying if said I've never done this. It took a few reminders from fire and EMS to help me remember not to do that. Well the same applies for police officers when it comes to a dynamic shooting scene. Make sure on an Active Shooter scene you're parking far enough away to allow law enforcement personnel to be able to access the scene. Our job is to take out the shooter and establish a safe perimeter as quick as possible. Blocking our routes with fire trucks and ambulances makes are job more difficult – and dangerous.

Also, do you have a member that loves talking on the radio? (We have those people in law enforcement too.) During a rapidly evolving active shooter event, we would all serve each other better if we keep radio traffic to a minimum (i.e., only transmit the most essential information). Early on, the scene is going to be chaotic and confusing. It is very important for law enforcement to keep lines of communication open and accessible. Non-essential chatter is distracting and can draw an officer's attention off-task and increase their risk.

Key Takeaways

Situational awareness is key for survival and saving as many lives as possible in an active shooter situation. Consider mentally rehearsing active shooter events thinking through, in advance, what your actions would be if you found yourself in that situation. Conducting simulated active shooter training (under stress) and practicing rapid response techniques, can improve a firefighter's and EMS crew member's ability to predict what may happen in these events and help you prevent bad outcomes.

Not all law enforcement officers have advanced training on how to handle an active shooter situation. Do not depend, entirely, on the officers to keep you safe. Use situational awareness best practices to improve the safety of your crew. (Here's a hint: There's more to situational awareness that paying attention and keeping your head on a swivel.) Be prepared to take quick action, if necessary.

One final note: According to the FBI, from the years 2000-2018, 98% of active shooter incidents had only one shooter. Statistically speaking, chances are your event will only be one shoote. However, there's always that chance there could be more than one. History also shows that when there are more than one shooter they are, most often, together. But, as you can imagine, there are no rules for active shooters to follow. Put yourself in the mindset that anything is possible and anything can happen.

Discussions

1. Discuss what you would do if an active shooter situation were to evolve unexpectedly during a fire or medical call.

2. Discuss how you could work more collaboratively with your local police departments to prepare, train and coordinate during active shooter events.

3. Discuss ways you could build stress into active shooter training to improve realism and to ensure you are prepared for the stress you will experience during an actual event.

Chapter 21

Active Shooter: The Citizen Response

If you find yourself at work, school, church, etc., when an active shooter event unfolds there are a few things you should know and practice. First, if you can safely do so, RUN! Get out of the situation as fast as possible. You will improve your chances of knowing where to run if, in advance, you are thinking about your way out far before you have to flee (think preplan). Once an event turns hostile, you will have little time to think about your escape route.

If running is not a safe option because the shooter is too close, then hide. I'm not talking about hiding under a desk. That, in fact, may be your worst option. Hiding under a desk makes you a sitting duck. Hiding under desks may work in the movies, but it's a bad plan in real life. Hiding means actively barricading yourself behind cover. If you cannot find cover, then find a way to conceal yourself.

Think of cover as a barrier that can stop bullets (e.g., the engine block of a car or a brick wall). Concealment, on the other hand, is something that will conceal (i.e., hide) your body, but bullets can still penetrate through (e.g., drywall or a wood door). When you hide, barricade and lock the door if possible. Put large heavy objects such as tables, computers, or desks in front of the door so it cannot easily be opened. Remain quiet and wait there as long as you need to until law enforcement arrives.

Lastly, and only if the first two options won't work, fight! If you are by yourself, your best option is to hurl any object available to you at the shooter and try to get away to cover or run out of the building. Use any means you can imagine to slow the shooter down. Active shooters are cowards and they won't be expecting a fight.

OODA Loop Disruption

One of the things we teach civilians on how to survive an active shooter encounter is to disrupt the shooters OODA loop. Let me explain. The OODA loop – developed by Air Force Colonel John Boyd – is a four-step decision making/action taking process. Colonel Boyd described it as:

(1) Observing;

(2) Orienting;

(3) Deciding; and,

(4) Acting.

By disrupting an Active Shooters decision making process (i.e., their OODA loop) we can momentarily cause the shooter to pause their decision making process and this may be all the advantage we need to increase our chance for survival.

For example, during a hockey game if the Forward is on a breakaway and has no Defender or Goalie in their path, they can OBSERVE there is no one to block their shot. The Forward can then ORIENT their stick in a way to ensure the shot can be made. The Forward can then DECIDE to shoot the puck into the empty net and ACT on that decision by slapping the puck toward the goal and score!

However, the entire process can be interrupted if there is a Defender facing the attacking Forward. If after Observing and Orienting, the Forward decides to shoot, the Defender may attempt to slap the puck away from the Forward. This maneuver may be enough to disrupt the Forward's decision making process (i.e., their OODA loop) and the Forward would likely avert the shot and start the OODA loop process over again. This can buy you a few precious seconds.

Think of the Flight 93 scenario, trained terrorists hijacked a plane. The passengers bonded together and took out the terrorists.

And while all the passengers perished when the plane crashed, their heroic actions likely saved countless lives at the destination the terrorists where intending to strike with the plane. They accomplished their mission by being brave, having a plan, and disrupting the terrorist's OODA Loop. They did a great job improvising weapons (e.g., a beverage cart, hot coffee).

Key Takeaways

Situational awareness is essential to your survival and may help save your life if you encounter an Active Shooter. Consider conducting mental rehearsals of Active Shooter scenarios. During a mental rehearsal, you imagine yourself in an Active Shooter situation and think through (in advance) what it would be like. Imagine using all of your senses. What would you be seeing, hearing, feeling, tasting and smelling? Vividly imagine the situation and how it would play out in as much detail as you can.

Practice "what if" decision making scenarios. For example, you might think: If I were in my office and I heard a gunshot in another part of the building, then I would _____ (fill in the blank). Rehearse as many "what if" scenarios as you can imagine, building complexity into the scenarios as you gain confidence.

The benefits of mental rehearsals can be two-fold. First, mental rehearsals can reduce surprises. Your critical thinking skills can be impacted by the element of surprise. (Coincidentally, disrupting critical thinking skills is what you're trying to accomplish when you interrupt the Active Shooter's OODA loop). When you find yourself in a real-world situation that you've mentally rehearsed, you're far less likely to be surprised. Rather, you'll be expecting it to happen and you will have already thought through one (or more) decision options.

The second benefit of mental rehearsals is they can help improve prediction skills. In active shooter situations, it is important that we are thinking ahead of the current situation – being mindful of not only what is happening right now, but also thinking about what is going to happen next (e.g., what/who might be waiting for me around the next corner?).

When practicing "if-then" scenarios and performing mental rehearsals, think beyond yourself. Imagine the actions of others who will be present. To take down an Active Shooter you may need to lead (direct) others on what to do. For workplace Active Shooter preparation, talk with coworkers about what should be done if an event occurs. The actions of your coworkers could help save lives. Or, their actions could cost lives. Don't assume everyone will know what to do. That would be a mistake. Have a plan! Remember, it's much easier for the body to get through a tough time when the mind has already experienced and planned for it.

Everyday Life

When we work with companies, we recommend annual training for all employees and the training cover all forms of potential violent acts at work. Professional training ensures workers know what to do, but also how to do it. Be prepared for an act of violence, this involves mental AND physical preparation.

Think about the phenomenal job firefighters have done teaching citizens how to Stop, Drop, and Roll if their clothing catches on fire. What to do is quite intuitive now, but it took years of repetitive training and having a plan for it to happen. Repetition improves physical and mental performance under stress. That's why schools conduct multiple fire drills every year. As a result of their diligent efforts, it is extremely rare for a student to die from a fire in a school.

We live in a world where, sadly, Active Shooter events are becoming more common. It's time for companies to develop plans and to take the lead training workers on how to be prepared.

Discussions

1. Discuss ways a person could disrupt an Active Shooter's OODA loop.

2. Discuss what objects in your home or at work could be used as a last-resort weapon to defend yourself against an active shoot.

3. Review and discuss your family's plan for an Active Shooter event.

4. Review and discuss your company's plan for an Active Shooter event.

5. Discuss with your coworkers what each of you should (and should not) do during an Active Shooter event.

Summary

This book was written for one purpose only – to help police officers, their supervisors, and their trainers understand how situational awareness is developed and maintained while working in high-risk, high-consequence, time-compressed environments.

To accomplish this goal, we hope we have been able to explain some of the complexities of situational awareness and its impact on decision making in friendly, easy to understand ways.

Our mission is to help police officers on the sharpest end of decision making see the bad things coming in time to prevent bad outcomes.

We hope your goal in reading this book was to accomplish your most important mission – to help you and those you work with go home from work, whole and healthy, every day, to the ones who love you/them.

If reading this book (or taking one of our courses) does not help you accomplish this goal, the investment of your time is wasted.

Conversely, if any police officer, supervisor or trainer is able to say they will look at high-risk work differently now then we have accomplished our goal and you're well on your way to being safer on the street.

To learn more about situational awareness
and high-risk decision making visit:

SAMatters.com

To schedule a consultation, a site assessment
or a training program contact us at:

Rich@RichGasaway.com

DMoldenhauer@SAMatters.com

612-548-4424

About the Authors

Richard B. Gasaway, PhD, CSP is widely considered a trusted authority on human factors, situational awareness and the high-risk decision making processes used in high-stress, high consequence work environments.

He served 33 years on the front lines as a firefighter, EMT-Paramedic, company officer, training officer, fire chief and emergency incident commander.

His doctoral research included the study of cognitive neuroscience to understand how human factors flaw situational awareness and impact high-risk decision making.

He is the founder and CEO for Situational Awareness Matters, a teaching and consulting organization located in Saint Paul, Minnesota. He can be reached at Rich@RichGasaway.com.

Drew W. Moldenhauer, M.S, has 15 years of Law Enforcement experience with two police organizations in Minnesota. Some of the titles he has held in his tenure are Active Shooter Instructor, Use of Force Instructor, Crisis Intervention Team (CIT) Instructor and Field Training Officer.

He is currently an Assistant Professor of Criminal Justice at Bemidji State University and is a full-time licensed police officer that works for the City of Osseo Police Department.

He holds a Master's Degree of Science in Public Safety Executive Leadership from St. Cloud State University. He is a Certified Master Instructor for Situational Awareness Matters and has a passion for training his clients on this very important subject. He can be reached at DMoldenhauer@SAMatters.com.

Made in the USA
Monee, IL
31 January 2023

a7bec8db-be58-4bf8-8ece-48b2a0d3fdeaR01